Success

Quote/Unquote

APPLEWOOD BOOKS
BEDFORD, MASSACHUSETTS

Copyright © 2002 Applewood Books, Inc.

Quotations Copyright © 2002 U-inspire, Inc.

*T*hank you for purchasing an Applewood Book. Applewood reprints America's lively classics—books from the past that are still of interest to modern readers. For a free copy of our current catalog, please write to Applewood Books, P.O. Box 365, Bedford, MA 01730

ISBN 1-55709-975-8

Library of Congress Control Number: 2001092157

10 9 8 7 6 5 4 3

Manufactured in U.S.A.

Introduction

Success ... it is the holy grail that we all seek. Whether it is on the job, on the field, in the community, at home or just at life in general ... we all want to be successful.

When creating this compilation we asked ourselves two questions. The first is, "What is success (and what isn't success)?" and the second is, "What does it take to succeed?" We endeavor to answer the first question in the "Quote" side of this collection by sharing quotations about the meaning of success. In the "Unquote" side of this collection, we endeavor to answer the second question by providing tips from experts throughout the ages on how to achieve success.

We think that individuals and organizations alike will benefit from this collection and we encourage you to share the insights that you find in this book. Most of all, we hope that you enjoy this collection and find the wisdom and motivation to achieve success in your life!

Quote

Success is following the pattern of life one enjoys most.

—Al Capp

Success is sweet and sweeter if long delayed and gotten through many struggles and defeats.

—Amos Bronson Alcott

In America, everything you need to succeed is within reach.

—Jim Rohn

Success

It is hard to fail, but it is worse never to have tried to succeed. In this life we get nothing save by effort.

— Theodore Roosevelt

Winning is not a sometime thing, it's an all time thing. You don't win once in a while, you don't do things right once in a while, you do them right all the time. Winning is habit. Unfortunately, so is losing.

— Vince Lombardi

The reward of a thing well done is to have done it.

— Ralph Waldo Emerson

𝒴ou always pass failure on the way to success.

— Mickey Rooney

𝓜ost people who succeed in the face of seemingly impossible conditions are people who simply don't know how to quit.

— Robert H. Schuller

𝒮uccess, or failure, very often arrives on wings that seem mysterious to us.

— Dr. Marcus Bach

Success

There is no point at which you can say, "Well, I'm successful now. I might as well take a nap."

— Carrie Fisher

Success isn't how far you got, but the distance you traveled from where you started.

— Source Unknown

Failure is a detour, not a dead-end street.

— Zig Ziglar

*S*uccess is to be measured not so much by the position that one has reached in life as by the obstacles which one has overcome while trying to succeed.

— Booker T. Washington

*S*uccess is not a harbor but a voyage with its own perils to the spirit. The game of life is to come up a winner, to be a success, or to achieve what we set out to do.

— Richard M. Nixon

I honestly think it is better to be a failure at something you love than to be a success at something you hate.

— George Burns

Success

The talent of success is nothing more than doing what you can do well, and doing well whatever you do.

— Henry Wadsworth Longfellow

Ninety-nine percent of the failures come from people who have the habit of making excuses.

— George Washington Carver

When you get into a tight place and everything goes against you, till it seems as though you could not hold on a minute longer, never give up then, for that is just the place and time that the tide will turn.

— Harriet Beecher Stowe

All human beings have failings, all human beings have needs and temptations and stresses. Men and women who live together through long years get to know one another's failings; but they also come to know what is worthy of respect and admiration in those they live with and in themselves. If at the end one can say, This man used to the limit the powers that God granted him; he was worthy of love and respect and of the sacrifices of many people, made in order that he might achieve what he deemed to be his task, then that life has been lived well and there are no regrets.

—Eleanor Roosevelt

People fail forward to success.

—Mary Kay Ash

Success is a journey, not a destination.

—Ben Sweetland

Success

You are not here to fritter away your precious hours when you have the ability to accomplish so much by making a slight change in your routine. No more hiding from success. Leave time, leave space, to grow. Now.

—Og Mandino

Before success in any man's life he is sure to meet with much temporary defeat and, perhaps, some failure. When defeat overtakes a man, the easiest and most logical thing to do is to quit. That is exactly what the majority of men do.

—Napoleon Hill

We want to be first; not first if, not first but; but first!

—John F. Kennedy

There is no happiness except in the realization that we have accomplished something.

— Henry Ford

I don't know the key to success, but the key to failure is trying to please everybody.

— Bill Cosby

Never continue in a job you don't enjoy. If you're happy in what you're doing, you'll like yourself, you'll have inner peace. And if you have that, along with physical health, you will have had more success than you could possibly have imagined.

— Johnny Carson

Success

The man who makes no mistakes does not usually make anything.

—Theodore Roosevelt

Keep in mind that neither success nor failure is ever final.

—Roger Babson

One's best success comes after their greatest disappointments.

—Henry Ward Beecher

Many of life's failures are people who did not realize how close they were to success when they gave up.

— Thomas A. Edison

Success is but a loose stone on the vast rocks of failure.

— Source Unknown

Success is a progressive realization of worthwhile, predetermined personal goals.

— Paul J. Meyer

Success

There is little success where there is little laughter.

—Andrew Carnegie

The twin killers of success are impatience and greed.

—Jim Rohn

Not many people are willing to give failure a second opportunity. They fail once and it is all over. The bitter pill of failure is often more than most people can handle. If you are willing to accept failure and learn from it, if you are willing to consider failure as a blessing in disguise and bounce back, you have got the essential of harnessing one of the most powerful success forces.

—Joseph Sugarman

Quote

There are two kinds of success. One is the very rare kind that comes to the man who has the power to do what no one else has the power to do. That is genius. But the average man who wins what we call success is not a genius. He is a man who has merely the ordinary qualities that he shares with his fellows, but who has developed those ordinary qualities to a more than ordinary degree.

— Theodore Roosevelt

Victory is sweetest when you've known defeat.

— Malcolm S. Forbes

If you have made mistakes, even serious ones, there is always another chance for you. What we call failure is not the falling down, but the staying down.

— Mary Pickford

Success

The road to success is always under construction.

— Lily Tomlin

Success is not to know the most about what you do, it is to do the most about what you don't know.

— Source Unknown

Men succeed when they realize that their failures are the preparation for their victories.

— Ralph Waldo Emerson

My great concern is not whether you have failed, but whether you are content with your failure.

—Abraham Lincoln

You may be disappointed if you fail, but you are doomed if you don't try.

—Beverly Sills

The only honest measure of your success is what you are doing compared to your true potential.

—Paul J. Meyer

Success

How many a man has thrown up his hands at a time when a little more effort, a little more patience would have achieved success.

— Elbert Hubbard

The minute you start talking about what you're going to do if you lose, you have lost.

— George Shultz

Success in its highest and noblest form calls for peace of mind and enjoyment and happiness which come only to the man who has found the work that he likes best.

— Napoleon Hill

When nothing seems to help, I'd look at one of my stonecutters hammering away at a rock, perhaps a hundred times without as much as a crack showing in it. Yet, at the hundred and first blow it would split in two, and I knew it was not that blow that did it, but all that had gone before.

—Jacob Riis

When all is said and done, success without happiness is the worst kind of failure.

—Louis Binstock

Each success only buys an admission ticket to a more difficult problem.

—Henry Kissinger

Success

When you get right down to the root meaning of the word "succeed" you find that it simply means to follow through.

— F. W. Nichol

Coming together is a beginning, staying together is progress and working together is success.

— Henry Ford

A man is a success if he gets up in the morning and gets to bed at night and in between he does what he wants to do.

— Bob Dylan

It's not whether you get knocked down, it's whether you get up.

— Vince Lombardi

The only failure a man ought to fear is failure in cleaving to the purpose he sees to be best.

— T. S. Eliot

Success without honor is an unseasoned dish; it will satisfy your hunger, but it won't taste good.

— Joe Paterno

Success

People who do not succeed have one distinguishing trait in common. They know all the reasons for failure and have what they believe to be air-tight alibis to explain their own lack of achievement.

— Napoleon Hill

Success is the prize for those who stand true to their ideas.

— Josh Hinds

Success doesn't mean the absence of failures; it means the attainment of ultimate objectives. It means winning the war, not every battle.

— Edwin C. Bliss

*P*rocrastination is the fear of success. People procrastinate because they are afraid of the success that they know will result if they move ahead now. Because success is heavy, carries a responsibility with it, it is much easier to procrastinate and live on the "someday I'll" philosophy.
— Denis Waitley

*H*owever things may seem, no evil thing is success and no good thing is failure.

— Henry Wadsworth Longfellow

*N*o one can possibly achieve any real and lasting success or "get rich" in business by being a conformist.

— J. Paul Getty

Success

Most people give up just when they're about to achieve success. They quit on the one yard line. They give up at the last minute of the game, one foot from a winning touchdown.

—H. Ross Perot

Where I was born and where and how I have lived is unimportant. It is what I have done with where I have been that should be of interest.

—Georgia O'Keeffe

That some achieve great success, is proof to all that others can achieve it as well.

—Abraham Lincoln

A failure is a man who has blundered, but is not able to cash in on the experience.

— Elbert Hubbard

*B*eing defeated is often a temporary condition. Giving up is what makes it permanent.

— Marilyn vos Savant

I firmly believe that any man's finest hour, the greatest fulfillment of all that he holds dear, is that moment when he has worked his heart out in a good cause and lies exhausted on the field of battle — victorious.

— Vince Lombardi

Success

---

*S*uccess is relevant to coping with obstacles . . . but no problem is ever solved by those, who, when they fail, look for someone to blame instead of something to do.

— Fred Waggoner

*S*uccess is always temporary. When all is said and done, the only thing you'll have left is your character.

— Vince Gill

*S*how me a thoroughly satisfied man and I will show you a failure.

— Thomas A. Edison

The Unquote

Everything comes to him who hustles while he waits.

— Henry Ford

I found that the men and women who got to the top were those who did the jobs they had in hand, with everything they had of energy and enthusiasm and hard work.

— Harry S Truman

The real secret of success is enthusiasm.

— Walter Chrysler

Success

Sweat plus sacrifice equals success.
— Charlie Finley

The most successful men in the end are those whose success is the result of steady accretion. It is the man who carefully advances step by step, with his mind becoming wider and wider — and progressively better able to grasp any theme or situation — persevering in what he knows to be practical, and concentrating his thought upon it, who is bound to succeed in the greatest degree.
— Alexander Graham Bell

The dictionary is the only place that success comes before work.
— Arthur Brisbane

If you want to increase your success rate, double your failure rate.

—Tom Watson

It had long since come to my attention that people of accomplishment rarely sat back and let things happen to them. They went out and happened to things.

—Elinor Smith

Success is a state of mind. If you want success, start thinking of yourself as a success.

—Dr. Joyce Brothers

Success

$\mathcal{G}$o forward confidently, energetically attacking problems, expecting favorable outcomes.

—Norman Vincent Peale

$\mathcal{S}$uccess is the result of perfection, hard work, learning from failure, loyalty, and persistence.

—Colin Powell

$\mathcal{D}$on't bother just to be better than your contemporaries or predecessors. Try to be better than yourself.

—William Faulkner

*D*o it now. You become successful the moment you start moving toward a worthwhile goal.

—Samuel Insull

*S*ome people dream of success...while others wake up and work hard at it.

—Source Unknown

*E*dison failed 10,000 times before he made the electric light. Do not be discouraged if you fail a few times.

—Napoleon Hill

Success

---

*E*ighty percent of success is showing up.

— Woody Allen

*S*uccess comes from taking the initiative and following up . . . persisting . . . eloquently expressing the depth of your love. What simple action could you take today to produce a new momentum toward success in your life?

— Tony Robbins

*S*uccess seems to be largely a matter of hanging on after others have let go.

— William Feather

Unquote

There is no chance, no destiny, no fate, that can circumvent or hinder or control the firm resolve of a determined soul.

—Ella Wheeler Wilcox

A little more persistence, a little more effort, and what seemed hopeless failure may turn to glorious success.

—Elbert Hubbard

Success seems to be connected with action. Successful men keep moving. They make mistakes, but they don't quit.

—Conrad Hilton

Success

We must walk consciously only part way toward our goal, and then leap in the dark to our success.

— Henry David Thoreau

I am not judged by the number of times I fail, but by the number of times I succeed: and the number of times I succeed is in direct proportion to the number of times I fail and keep trying.

— Tom Hopkins

Nothing splendid has ever been achieved except by those who dared believe that something inside them was superior to circumstance.

— Bruce Barton

*O*nly those who dare to fail greatly can ever achieve greatly.

— Robert F. Kennedy

*S*uccess in business requires training and discipline and hard work. But if you're not frightened by these things, the opportunities are just as great today as they ever were.

— David Rockefeller

*T*he person interested in success has to learn to view failure as a healthy, inevitable part of the process of getting to the top.

— Dr. Joyce Brothers

Success

Success usually comes to those who are too busy to be looking for it.

— Henry David Thoreau

Press on: nothing in the world can take the place of perseverance. Talent will not; nothing is more common than unsuccessful men with talent. Genius will not; unrewarded genius is almost a proverb. Education will not; the world is full of educated derelicts. Persistence and determination alone are omnipotent.

— Calvin Coolidge

If A equals success, then the formula is: $A=X+Y+Z$. X is work. Y is play. Z is keep your mouth shut.

— Albert Einstein

If you want to succeed you should strike out on new paths rather than travel the worn paths of accepted success.

— John D. Rockefeller, Jr.

For you to be successful, sacrifices must be made. It's better that they are made by others but failing that, you'll have to make them yourself.

— Rita Mae Brown

Nothing can stop the man with the right mental attitude from achieving his goal; nothing on earth can help the man with the wrong mental attitude.

— Thomas Jefferson

Success

𝒯o be successful, the first thing to do is fall in love with your work.

—Sister Mary Lauretta

𝒪ne essential to success is that your desire be an all-obsessing one, your thoughts and aims be co-ordinated, and your energy be concentrated and applied without letup.

—Claude M. Bristol

𝒫eople with goals succeed because they know where they're going.

—Earl Nightingale

Unquote

No one gets an iron-clad guarantee of success. Certainly, factors like opportunity, luck and timing are important. But the backbone of success is usually found in old fashioned, basic concepts like hard work, determination, good planning and perseverance.

— Merlin Olsen

Success is often the result of taking a misstep in the right direction.

— Al Bernstein

Aim for the highest.

— Andrew Carnegie

Success

$\mathscr{V}$ictory is always possible for the person who refuses to stop fighting.

— Napoleon Hill

$\mathscr{A}$ competitor will find a way to win. Competitors take bad breaks and use them to drive themselves just that much harder. Quitters take bad breaks and use them as reasons to give up. It's all a matter of pride.

— Nancy Lopez

$\mathscr{T}$he most important single ingredient in the formula of success is knowing how to get along with people.

— Theodore Roosevelt

I hated every minute of training, but I said, "Don't quit. Suffer now and live the rest of your life as a champion."

—Muhammad Ali

*C*ommit yourself to a dream. Nobody who tries to do something great but fails is a total failure. Why? Because he can always rest assured that he succeeded in life's most important battle—he defeated the fear of trying.

—Robert H. Schuller

*T*o succeed in business it is necessary to make others see things as you see them.

—John H. Patterson

Success

Hold yourself responsible to a higher standard than anybody else expects of you; never excuse yourself.

— Henry Ward Beecher

Most of the successful people I've known are the ones who do more listening than talking.

— Bernard M. Baruch

You can have anything you want—if you want it badly enough. You can be anything you want to be, do anything you set out to accomplish if you hold to that desire with singleness of purpose.

— Abraham Lincoln

The victory of success is half done when one gains the habit of work.

— Sarah Knowles Bolton

Success follows doing what you want to do. There is no other way to be successful.

— Malcolm S. Forbes

A man can succeed at almost anything for which he has unlimited enthusiasm.

— Charles M. Schwab

Success

Forget mistakes. Forget failure. Forget everything except what you're going to do now, and do it.

—Will Durant

I do not think that there is any other quality so essential to success of any kind as the quality of perseverance. It overcomes almost everything, even nature.

—John D. Rockefeller

Persistent people begin their success where others end in failure.

—Edward Eggleston

*D*o not be discouraged if your plans do not succeed the first time. No one learns to walk by taking only one step.

—Catherine Pulsifer

*O*f course there is no formula for success except perhaps an unconditional acceptance of life and what it brings.

—Artur Rubinstein

*A*verage people look for ways of getting away with it; successful people look for ways of getting on with it.

—Jim Rohn

Success

$\mathscr{A}$bility may get you to the top, but it takes character to keep you there.

—John Wooden

$\mathscr{T}$o keep our faces toward change, and behave like free spirits in the presence of fate, is strength undefeatable.

—Helen Keller

$\mathscr{S}$uccess is not the result of spontaneous combustion. You must set yourself on fire.

—Source Unknown

One important key to success is self-confidence. An important key to self-confidence is preparation.

— Arthur Ashe

Plan to succeed, or you have planned to fail.

— Donald Hall

The difference between a successful person and others is not a lack of strength, not a lack of knowledge, but rather is a lack of will.

— Vince Lombardi

Flaming enthusiasm, backed by horse sense and persistence, is the quality that most frequently makes for success.

— Dale Carnegie

If I had to select one quality, one personal characteristic that I regard as being most highly correlated with success, whatever the field, I would pick the trait of persistence. Determination. The will to endure to the end, to get knocked down seventy times and get up off the floor saying, "Here comes number seventy-one!"

— Richard M. DeVos

Believe and act as if it were impossible to fail.

— Charles F. Kettering

Unquote

I know the price of success: dedication, hard work, and a devotion to things you want to see happen.

—Frank Lloyd Wright

*T*he secret of getting ahead is getting started. The secret of getting started is breaking your complex overwhelming tasks into small manageable tasks, and then starting on the first one.

—Mark Twain

*S*uccess comes from knowing that you did your best to become the best that you are capable of becoming.

—John Wooden

Success

$\mathcal{M}$any times the difference between failure and success is doing something nearly right . . . or doing it exactly right.

—Source Unknown

$\mathcal{T}$he great successful men of the world have used their imaginations, they think ahead and create their mental picture, and then go to work materializing that picture in all its details, filling in here, adding a little there, altering this a bit and that bit, but steadily building, steadily building.

—Robert Collier

$\mathcal{S}$uccess is dependent upon the glands —sweat glands.

—Zig Ziglar

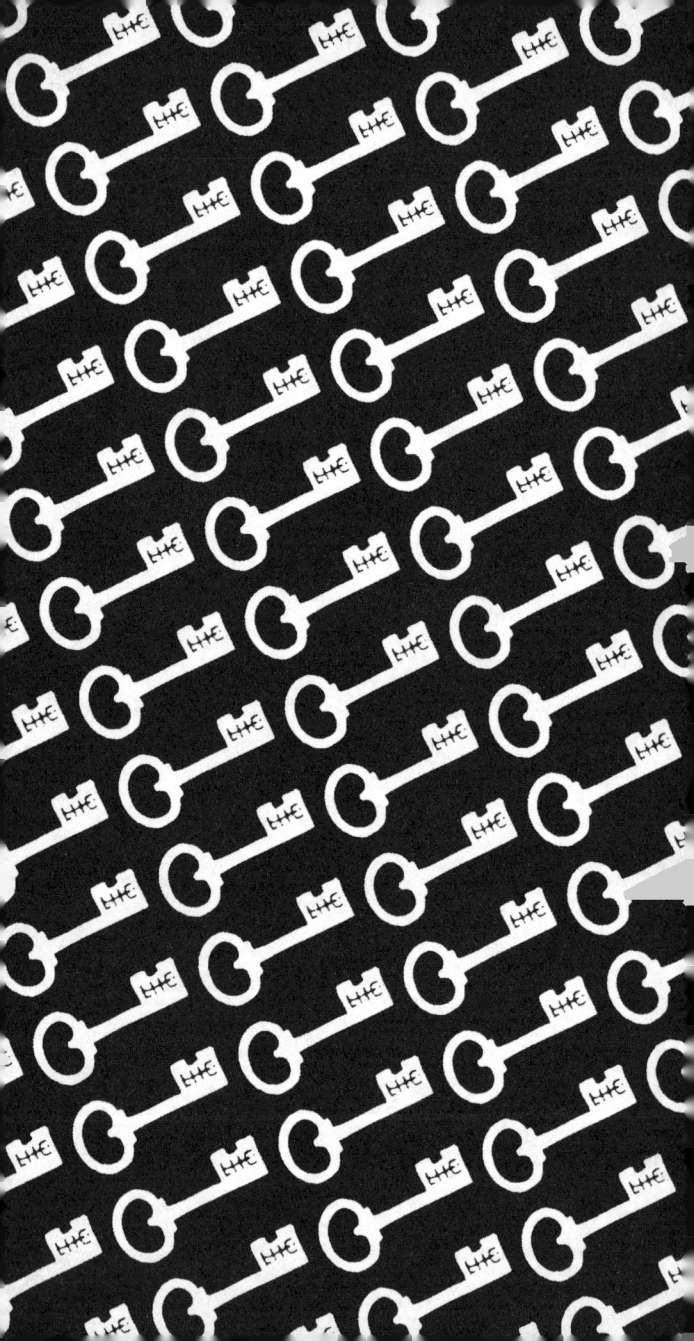